TANGO
AT THE END
OF WINTER

KUNIO SHIMIZU

TANGO
AT THE END
OF WINTER

ADAPTED BY
PETER BARNES

AMBER LANE PRESS

All rights whatsoever in this play are strictly reserved and
application for performance, etc. must be made before
rehearsals begin to:

Margaret Ramsay Ltd.
14a Goodwin's Court
St Martins Lane
London WC2N 4LL

No performance may be given unless a licence has been
obtained.

First published in 1991 by
Amber Lane Press Ltd
Cheorl House
Church Street
Charlbury, Oxon OX7 3PR

Telephone: 0608 810024

Typeset in Garamond by
Oxonian Rewley Press Ltd, Oxford

Printed by Great Britain by
Bocardo Press Ltd, Didcot, Oxfordshire

ISBN 1 872868 05 3

Tango at the End of Winter was first presented by Thelma Holt Limited and Point Tokyo Co. Ltd. (and sponsored by the Great Britain-Sasakawa Foundation) at the King's Theatre, Edinburgh, as part of the Edinburgh Festival on 10th August 1991. The play received its London premiere at the Piccadilly Theatre on 28th August 1991 and was presented by arrangement with Triumph Proscenium Productions Ltd. It was directed by Yukio Ninagawa with the following cast:

SEI:	Alan Rickman
GIN:	Suzanne Bertish
SHIGEO:	Robert Glenister
NOBUKO:	Anne Marie Cavanah
HANA:	Diana Fairfax
MIZUO:	Beatie Edney
REN:	Barry Stanton
TAMAMI:	Mandy Cheshire
TOUTA:	Rupert Mason
UNCLE KAMIHIDA:	Peter Bayliss
UNCLE KITAHIDA:	Peter Whitbread
COUSIN NISHIHIDA:	Timothy Bateson

Other parts played by:
Sybil Allen, Bruce Bennett, Jonathan Butterell,
Richard Clothier, Paul Crosby,
Sheila Shand Gibbs, Philip Pellew,
Stuart Pendred, Simon Penman, Jerome Turner
and Jason Webb.

Set Design by Setsu Asakura
Costume Design by Lily Komine
Lighting Design by Sumio Yoshii
Sound Design by Akira Honma
Choreography by Glenn Wright
English translation by Stefan Kaiser and Sue Henny

CHARACTERS

KIYOMURA SEI
GIN (Sei's wife)
SHIGEO (Sei's brother)
MIYAKOSHI NOBUKO (receptionist and cleaner)
KIYOMURA HANA (aunt to Sei and Shigeo)
NAWA MIZUO
NAWA REN (Mizuo's husband)
TAMAMI (a schoolgirl)
TOUTA (a schoolboy)
UNCLE KAMIHIDA (a policeman)
UNCLE KITAHIDA
COUSIN NISHIHIDA

The action takes place in a cinema
in a northern town of Japan.
It is spring and the time is the present.

9

ACT ONE

Prologue

Darkness. Heavy breathing. Lights half up on a cinema, packed with young men and women, watching a film.

The cinema audience roar with laughter at the heavy breathing coming from the screen [off] . . . then they sigh . . . then a gasp of excitement as a war scene appears on the screen.

Sound of gunfire, flashes and explosions. The gasps of excitement turn to screams as the screen guns are turned onto the cinema audience. As they die the seats are stained with blood.

Blackout.

Scene One

Lush film music. Lights slowly up on the cinema, which looks old and broken down.

The audience is still there but we see that they are actually life-size cardboard cut-outs.

Asleep in the middle of them is KIYOMURA SEI.

Lights flood in as GIN, SEI's *wife, enters, stage left. She is dressed as if she is going on a journey. She moves downstage centre and addresses the audience directly.*

GIN: This is where my husband was born. He spent most of his youth in this cinema. There's a living area at the back. The room my husband used to study in as a child was just over there . . .

[*She points. Film music creeps in.*]

I arrived here three years ago, in April. That's still the end of winter this far north. When I stepped down onto the station platform I could actually hear the Sea of Japan there in the distance. I never realised it was that close . . . I came here looking for my husband. He'd suddenly left Tokyo, given up everything and shut himself away in this remote place. He's an actor — or was. Very talented. People still talk about him . . . I remember, the day I arrived there was this hoarding advertising *Rocky 2* — or was it *3*? — anyway, it was broken and it was being battered by the wind . . . bang, bang . . . bang, bang, bang . . .

> [*Lights change and* GIN *crosses to* SEI, *who opens his eyes. They glare at each other. Then* GIN *raises her hand.*]

Hello.

SEI: [*raising his hand*] Hello . . .

> [*This is obviously some sort of private signal between husband and wife.* GIN *looks at the cardboard cut-outs.*]

Don't worry, they're friends of mine.

GIN: Friends?

SEI: The best . . . [*raising his hand*] Hello . . .

GIN: [*raising her hand*] Hello . . .

SEI: "In life there are times of fire."

GIN: "And times of boredom."

SEI: That's it.

GIN: "I have an empty feeling in my stomach . . . "

SEI: "But my heart is full."

GIN: What play did those lines come from?

SEI: I don't know.

GIN: Why is it always easier to remember bad lines than good?

SEI: [*raising his hand; softly*] Hello . . .

> [GIN *sits down beside him.*]

GIN: [*raising her hand*] Hello . . .

SEI: Let's watch the movie . . .

[*He puts his arm around* GIN, *drawing her closer.*]

How many years is it since we watched a film together like this?

[*He turns towards the projection room, upstage.*]

OK, we're ready!

GIN: [*turning upstage*] I don't think there's anyone up there.

SEI: Oh yes there is. He's hiding in the shadows. I know. [*pointing to his head*] He's a bit funny up here. He keeps running films even though there's no-one to watch 'em except these stupid cut-outs. He made them all, you know. [*turning round again*] Hey! Show us something. Even if it's only *Rocky*. [*turning back*] That's a great love story. Come on! We're waiting.

[*The voice of* SEI's *brother,* SHIGEO, *is heard, shouting from the projection room.*]

SHIGEO: [*off*] I haven't got *Rocky* any more.

SEI: That's my brother . . .

GIN: I know.

SEI: Faithful to the end. [*shouting up to the projection room*] Anything'll do!

SHIGEO: [*off*] I haven't got anything.

SEI: This is your big brother talking to you now!

SHIGEO: [*off*] Stop it!

SEI: We mustn't let the lights of the Northern Metropole go out forever!

GIN: Darling, please . . .

SEI: My brother needs encouraging . . . Shigeo!

[*As* SEI *runs up the steps and disappears upstage, one of the cardboard cut-outs comes to life and walks downstage. It is* SHIGEO.]

SHIGEO: He said I'm funny in the head, didn't he? Running films even though there's nobody here to watch them.

GIN: Yes.

SHIGEO: I'm doing it for him. It's all for his sake. Even these stupid puppets I made for him so he wouldn't feel so lonely.

> [SEI*'s voice is heard, chanting "Shigeo!"* SHIGEO *hurries off, stage left.*]

> [*Film music sweeps up as* GIN *talks to the audience.*]

GIN: My husband seemed just the same as before. Cheerful . . . then irritated . . . But I felt his pain. I thought he was going to get worse . . . After a year I knew I was right.

> [SEI *enters, stage left, with a rug draped around him like a gown, and dragging his feet.*]

What happened, darling?

SEI: They shot me.

GIN: Who?

SEI: How should I know? I suddenly started going numb all over.

GIN: No, you haven't been shot.

SEI: Could've been a tranquillising gun. The kind they use on wild animals.

GIN: Impossible . . . who'd have a gun like that?

SEI: Do something! I can't move my legs!

GIN: All right . . . come here . . . now relax . . . breathe deeply . . . breathe deeply . . .

SEI: Wait a minute, why am I breathing deeply? It's not my lungs, it's my legs that won't move!

GIN: Just do it.

SEI: Never. I refuse to do anything so unscientific. Breathing's got nothing to do with legs.

GIN: Please.

SEI: All right . . . just this once.

> [SEI *takes a deep breath.*]

GIN: Deeper . . . deeper . . .

> [SEI *continues to breathe deeply. Then his right leg twitches and jerks forward, then his left leg. He lurches about, stiff-legged.*]

SEI: It's a miracle, doctor! I can walk! . . . Who're you?

GIN: Don't you remember? Last summer you had exactly the same symptoms . . .

SEI: I did?

GIN: But it was in the middle of the night that time . . . I didn't know what to do so I just kept massaging your legs . . . and suddenly there was a big yawn.

SEI: You were tired.

GIN: Not me, you! . . . You yawned . . . and then you could move your legs.

SEI: A miracle . . . Don't tell anyone about this.

GIN: Why not?

SEI: People might think I'm simple-minded — or worse.

GIN: On the other hand it might make you even more of a legend.

SEI: The phone's ringing.

GIN: Where?

SEI: In the office.

GIN: I can't hear it.

SEI: It's probably the same lot as before.

GIN: What lot?

SEI: The ones who keep trying to get me to stage a comeback.

GIN: No, that stopped months ago. It's true up to then you had all kinds of offers but you turned them all down . . . People get tired of asking . . . they give up.

SEI: It's ringing again. It's them.

GIN: Why don't you answer it, then?

SEI: No, no, I don't want to! Even if I did it wouldn't make any difference. I've no intention of making a comeback. Never . . . Still, the members of my old company won't give up easily. I know them. We had a special relationship . . . we were a real company . . . friends who faced life together, who lived through difficult times and triumphed . . . When I left it was the end. That's why they can't let go . . . they want me back . . . don't you think? Why don't you say something? You're not trying to tell me they've forgotten me, are you?

GIN: Oh, no.

SEI: Good.

GIN: After all, you were the star . . . their inspiration, the one they put on a pedestal . . .

SEI: Yes . . . but people on pedestals are exposed to the wind and the rain, aren't they? They fade, bits fall off . . .

GIN: Come on, darling. You're tired.

SEI: Why do you lie these days?

GIN: Why do you?

> [*They glare at each other for a moment.*]

SEI: [*raising his hand*] Hello . . .

GIN: [*raising her hand*] Hello . . .

SEI: OK, let's go . . .

> [*He tries to walk.*]

You see, they don't move.

> [*He staggers.*]

GIN: Darling . . .

SEI: Don't look at me like that! You think I'm imagining it all . . . maybe you're right. Maybe I am imagining it all and there's nothing wrong with my legs. My body's still young even if my legs aren't. I could still play Hamlet or Romeo . . . if I wanted to. Look, look, they're moving! They're moving.

> [*He walks with increasing confidence.*]

I feel like dancing. My leg'll dance for you right now if you like.

> [*He dances.*]

GIN: Stop it.

SEI: No, nothing will stop my legs now! . . . What was that play we did? The one about those young men in the Resistance . . . I've forgotten the story . . . can't even remember what period it was set in . . . or who they were resisting.

GIN: We danced the tango, didn't we?

SEI: That's right. We danced the tango . . . of course, you were in it too!

GIN: I was just a member of the cast. You played the lead . . .

SEI: Naturally.

GIN: There was a good scene at the end when all those young men on their last day say goodbye before they go to their deaths in some forgotten cause.

> [SEI *stands on an imaginary stage. Spotlight on him.*]

SEI: "Goodbye . . . this is our last goodbye . . . we remain true to ourselves to the end . . . We tried to resist oppression and injustice and we failed . . . but there's honour in that failure. Now we wait for our end . . . to be taken out and shot . . . Yet I feel so calm. I can hardly believe how calm I feel. Someone is playing a tango, far, far away."

> [*A tango is heard playing.*]

When I hear a tango I think of freedom and revolution . . . and what my life has been . . . pictures from the past . . . Look . . . a white road in the morning . . . newspapers scattered by the wind like cherry blossom . . . lanterns someone forgot to turn off . . . schoolboys drinking water from a cup on a chain . . . and all those people . . . those who cheered . . . those who applauded . . . those who loved me . . .

> [*A group of* MEN *and* WOMEN *from* SEI*'s past appear between the seats, with black shawls around their shoulders. They laugh silently and wave their hands and flap their arms like birds.*]

I'm going to dance . . . take my hand . . . quick, quick.

> [SEI *climbs the steps and tries to get near the* PHANTOMS *wrapped in their shawls. But he trips and falls.*]

GIN: Darling . . .

> [*She runs up to* SEI *The* PHANTOMS *disappear and* SHIGEO *enters, upstage.*]

Help me, Shigeo.

SHIGEO: What happened?

GIN: Nothing. He was just remembering a play he did.

> [*They raise* SEI *to his feet.*]

SHIGEO: Stand up, slowly.

SEI: Who're you?

SHIGEO: What're you talking about? It's me.

SEI: Me? Oh yes, it's you.

SHIGEO: Lean on me . . .
          [They come downstage.]

SEI: That's good. I can feel that warmth you can only get from your brother or sister . . . isn't that right, sister?

GIN: Sister?

SEI: Yes, you're my sister, aren't you?

SHIGEO: He's a bit confused today.

SEI: I remember how I used to be scolded . . . Hey, Sei, what're you doing sitting alone in the dark? . . . Isn't he weird? He's dreaming with his eyes open . . . he must be sick . . . Oh, I haven't forgotten that, sister, I haven't forgotten how you used to scold me . . .
          [GIN detaches herself from SEI, leaving SHIGEO to help him alone.]

SHIGEO: We'd better put him to bed, he's exhausted . . .
          [SHIGEO carries SEI off, stage left.]
          [Film music. GIN turns to the audience.]

GIN: Like Shigeo, I thought it was only temporary and all he needed was to sleep. But he never woke from that dream. A year later I'm still his sister . . .
          [Lights fade down.]
          When I was in high school I used to play truant and go to the movies . . . and I'd have this extraordinary experience. After spending the best part of the day in the cinema I'd come out . . . and I couldn't find my way home, I was completely lost. I have that same sort of feeling now. If I go outside I can't find my way back . . . If I stay in here I'm all right. I can live in this dream. Or at least I tell myself it is only a dream . . . but I still have to fight to believe it . . .
          [Darkness.]

Scene Two

Lights half up.

A year later. The end of winter. The same cinema. Lying between the seats is a dazzling white dead body, which turns out to be a naked mannequin.

MIYAKOSHI NOBUKO, *the receptionist and cleaner, enters, stage left, carrying a mop. She short-sightedly bumps into the mannequin and moves it out of the way.*

Lights full up as SHIGEO *and his aunt,* KIYOMURA HANA, *enter upstage centre.* KIYOMURA HANA *is carrying a large bag. She points to the mannequin.*

HANA: What's that?

SHIGEO: Nobuko, what the devil's that?

NOBUKO: What, sir?

SHIGEO: That.

NOBUKO: I don't know.

SHIGEO: It's probably left over from one of the bridal sales we've been holding. I wonder how it got here.

HANA: Yes, the wedding season is on us again. How much do you charge for renting the cinema out?

           [SHIGEO *watches* NOBUKO *pick up the mannequin.*]

SHIGEO: It varies . . . Careful . . . careful . . .

NOBUKO: May as well take it with me as nobody seems to want it.

           [NOBUKO *exits, stage left.*]

HANA: She's been with you quite some time, hasn't she?

SHIGEO: Her sight's so bad nobody else'd take her on.

HANA: I haven't been here for years. It looks terrible. Much worse than I imagined . . . What's that smell?

SHIGEO: Smell?

HANA: Yes, smell. You sure there isn't something dead under the floorboards?

SHIGEO: I don't think so.

HANA: What about damp? That's worse. It's the one thing you have to be really careful about. If it's here, get rid of it before we start construction work in the summer.

SHIGEO: All right.

HANA: I'm glad you finally made up your mind. I think your poor, dear father would've been pleased. After all, this way the cinema stays in the family. What does Sei think?

SHIGEO: I haven't told him yet.

HANA: You'll have to tell him sooner or later . . . And you'll have to do something about him . . . By the way, don't worry about a place for the two of them to live. Leave it to me. I've already found a house for them.

SHIGEO: Could you find something for me? A flat'd do fine.

HANA: It's all taken care of. I am your aunt, after all. You can live here. I'm thinking of building flats above the supermarket for the employees. I've earmarked a place for you, you'll be helping in the supermarket, so it's only right.

SHIGEO: They're not communal flats, are they? I'm a bit too old to be sharing rooms.

HANA: No, they're private. Of course, you'll be living with Kayo and me whilst they're being built. The house is much too big. Kayo misses her father. It's hard bringing up a daughter alone. When I told her you'd be staying with us she was very pleased.

SHIGEO: Oh, yes.

HANA: She's quite slim these days. She's lost a good ten pounds.

SHIGEO: Ten pounds? You mean she's under fifteen stone now?

HANA: Almost . . .

[*She takes out a packet of cigarettes, then looks around.*]

Oh, it's no smoking, isn't it?

SHIGEO: It doesn't make much difference now, does it?

HANA: You're right . . . It's all a bit sad, though. Finally having to pull the old place down. How long has it been since you took over?

SHIGEO: Eight years.

HANA: That long? You've been really unlucky being landed with this monstrosity . . . Your elder brother becomes an actor, the second and third die young . . . and so your father forces you to carry on the family tradition and manage the cinema. What a tradition! . . . I suppose you'd rather have kept teaching?

SHIGEO: No, I rather liked running a cinema.

HANA: I wonder just how many films I saw here?

SHIGEO: What was your favourite?

HANA: Hard to say. There were so many . . . I think *Limelight* . . . yes, *Limelight*. The Chaplin film. That was good. Remember the scene where Chaplin is encouraged by the ballerina he helped when she was down on her luck? The girl has bad legs but forced herself to walk. Now she tells him to do the same or something like that. I forget the scene exactly . . .

SHIGEO: Chaplin has lost all hope and says to Terry — that's the ballerina — "I'm not going back on stage." So Terry says something like, "Why?" And Chaplin says, "Because they've just cancelled my contract, I'm finished!" "Nonsense, Calvero," says Terry . . . Calvero is the name of the Chaplin character . . . "Nonsense, Calvero. Don't let this destroy you, you're too great an artist. Now is the time to fight! Remember what you once told me about the power of the universe moving the earth, making mountains, valleys, trees. Now's the time to use that power! Look, I'm walking, Calvero! I'm walking! . . . I'm walking! . . . Calvero, I'm walking!"

HANA: Oh yes . . . that's the scene . . .

SHIGEO: Actually, I don't really like Chaplin. Too sentimental for me . . .

HANA: If you're that enthusiastic about films you dislike, what about the ones you like?

SHIGEO: I like Westerns.

HANA: You're a boy, it's natural.

SHIGEO: I like Western heroines best of all. They're part of a fixed unchanging pattern, that's what I like about them. The stage coach arrives in a cloud of dust. All the townsfolk are out to meet it. And the heroine steps down from the coach in a white dress. Always a white dress. Never dirty, never soiled, always white. You see her controlling her fear as she goes to the saloon to get news of her husband or lover. We suddenly cut to the saloon bar. The baddies in black are drinking whisky and playing poker at a nearby table . . . the men sense something . . . Pushing up the brows of their stetsons with one finger they turn and look . . . and as if in a dream there in the entrance stands a woman in white . . .

[SHIGEO *turns round and there, upstage centre, stands a woman dressed in white.*]

[*The young woman,* NAWA MIZUO, *comes down the aisle as* SHIGEO *and* HANA *recover.*]

Hello . . .

MIZUO: I'm looking for Kiyomura Sei — the actor . . .

SHIGEO: That's my brother. He isn't here at the moment . . . He always goes for a walk in the afternoon.

MIZUO: I thought he was ill.

[SHIGEO *and* HANA *exchange glances.*]

HANA: Yes he is, in a way.

SHIGEO: He should be here in half an hour.

MIZUO: I'll come back, then.

HANA: Are you from Tokyo?

MIZUO: Yes.

HANA: Why don't you wait here?

MIZUO: No, it's all right.

[*She bows slightly and exits, stage left.*]

HANA: Who is she?

SHIGEO: No idea.

[MIZUO *returns, very flustered.*]

MIZUO: There's somebody outside I don't want to see . . . Is there another exit?

SHIGEO: This way . . .

> [*At that moment* NOBUKO *appears, stage right, carrying a bucket.*]

Nobuko, please show this lady to the back door.

> [MIZUO *exits with* NOBUKO, *stage right.*]

HANA: What's going on?

> [NAWA REN, *carrying a paper bag and wearing a thick coat, enters, stage left. He looks around.*]

SHIGEO: Can I help you?

REN: Was there a woman in here just now?

SHIGEO: No.

REN: This is the only cinema in town, isn't it?

SHIGEO: Yes, but we're closed down.

> [REN *drops into a seat.*]

REN: Can I wait?

SHIGEO: For what?

REN: Don't worry, I won't cause any trouble. Do you mind if I eat a sandwich? I bought two on the train . . . [*opens the bag*] I've got some apples and oranges too . . . [*holds up an apple*] Bought it in Norgano . . . look how red it is . . . I wonder if it's as good as ones from Aomori . . .

SHIGEO: No, no, this won't do.

REN: Won't do. Why?

SHIGEO: Well . . . because we aren't showing any films.

REN: I didn't come here to see films.

HANA: But this is a cinema.

REN: It's closed.

SHIGEO: I know. But it still won't do.

REN: Please let me wait.

> [REN *is crying.* SHIGEO *and* HANA *do not know what to do, as* GIN *enters, upstage right.*]

GIN: Hello, I'm back. It started snowing so I thought it'd be better for Sei if we came back early.

HANA: It's like that here. It can snow right up to the time the cherry blossoms fall.

GIN: Thank you for the present.

HANA: It's nothing . . . Where is Sei?

GIN: In his room . . . He keeps picking up pebbles on the beach . . . like a child . . .

[*She suddenly notices* REN *slumped in a seat and looks enquiringly at* SHIGEO, *who is about to speak when* REN *jumps up.*]

REN: Hello, it's been a long time.

GIN: Ren!

[REN *hesitates then offers her an apple.*]

REN: Would you like an apple?

GIN: What?

REN: It's from Norgano.

GIN: Oh yes . . . Thank you . . .

HANA: You know each other?

[NOBUKO *enters, stage left.*]

NOBUKO: There's a telephone call . . . from Aunt Shimohida.

HANA: For me. I didn't realise it was that late . . . Must go, duty calls . . . Oh Shigeo, just a quick word . . .

[HANA *and* SHIGEO *exit, stage left, whispering.*]

REN: To tell the truth, I didn't want to see you.

GIN: Me? Or him?

REN: Both of you.

GIN: You haven't changed.

REN: If I were a baseball pitcher I'd only pitch straight ball — straight and fast. At least that's what everybody says. Actually, I can pitch crooked balls too when I want to.

GIN: Why are you here?

REN: I came after Mizuo . . . Why not? She's my wife.

GIN: She's not here.

REN: She got a letter from Sei.

GIN: He's written to her? . . . What kind of letter?

REN: I don't know. I didn't read it. It was probably something like "I must see you" . . . that's the impression I got judging by the note she left me.

GIN: So what did you do?

REN: I went straight after her, of course. I caught up with her on the train but she asked me to leave her alone for a few days and she promised she'd come back to me . . . So we ended up getting off separately at the station and when I was buying some food she disappeared . . .

[SEI *is heard singing, off.* REN *reacts.*]

GIN: It's him.

REN: So it's true. He's quite bad?

GIN: Yes. The difference between his good days and his bad days is getting worse. He can't remember faces. I went to see this doctor about it and he said he has a hatred for people.

REN: That's not much help. Does he sing on his good days or his bad days?

GIN: It depends.

REN: [*listening*] Sounds like one of his bad days . . . I wonder if he'll recognise me.

[SEI *enters upstage, singing. He stops when he sees* GIN *and* REN *and sticks his hand inside his shirt.*]

SEI: "As a boy he was uncommunicative and disobedient. As a young man arrogant and unmanageable. As an old man cheerful and whimsical."

GIN: What're you doing now?

SEI: Napoleon.

GIN: Oh yes. So what you just said were Napoleon's words?

SEI: Did they sound Napoleonic?

GIN: Yes.

SEI: Well, they weren't. Just a poem. I said it in the Napoleonic manner. You see how easy it is to fool people? Why did he stick his hand inside his shirt? Probably had an itch. He was always scratching himself. Still, it's interesting. You put your hand in your shirt like this and you immediately become Napoleon. Try it.

[REN *thrusts his hand in his shirt.*]

Are you itchy?

REN: No.

SEI: So why are you scratching yourself?

REN: [*taking his hand away*] I'm Nawa Ren. We haven't seen you for a long time.

SEI: Hello . . .

REN: [*aside to* GIN] He hasn't changed at all in three years . . . looks as young as ever . . .

SEI: No. No, no, no. If you're going to do asides you must do them clearly — so the audience can hear. It's not naturalism — it's acting. Try again.

REN: [*aside to* GIN *but louder*] He hasn't changed at all in three years . . . looks as young as ever . . .

SEI: Better.

REN: Thanks.

SEI: My hands are sticky. [*to* GIN] Have you got a handkerchief?

      [GIN *gives him a handkerchief.*]

      Perhaps doing Napoleon was a bit over the top . . . I just wanted to give the audience something extra.

GIN: Audience? What audience?

SEI: [*indicating* REN] Him . . . You see they've finally arrived. Without warning. Trying to throw me off balance! But it won't work! Never!

GIN: Darling . . .

SEI: Don't worry, I'm perfectly calm . . . [*to* REN] I don't like small talk of any kind, so would you kindly leave?

REN: But I only just got here.

SEI: I didn't ask you to come. I've told you before. I've no intention of making a comeback.

REN: Comeback? I didn't . . .

GIN: Please remember what I said . . .

REN: Oh yes . . . no comeback . . . I understand . . . if that's the way you feel I'll never mention it again.

SEI: Thank you . . . no comeback.

REN: No comeback.

SEI: [*irritably*] You didn't try very hard, did you?

      [GIN *signals* REN *to play along.*]

REN: Didn't I? . . . Well, it might seem I've given up very easily but I haven't. It's just my way. I'm still optimistic you'll change your mind.

SEI: "Here is my journey's end, here is my butt. / And very sea-mark of my utmost sail. / Do you go back dismayed? 'tis a lost fear; / Man but a rush against Othello's breast, / And he retires. / Where should Othello go?" . . . You saw my Othello?

REN: Of course. I was even there on the last night.

SEI: So you heard me announce I was going to retire.

REN: We all thought it was wonderful. Wonderful . . . I mean it was extraordinary . . . never heard anything so dramatic . . . [*quoting*] "Ladies and gentlemen, the beautiful should die young, let others live as long as they can . . . "

   [*He stops, embarrassed.*]

SEI: No, no, carry on. It's good.

REN: Ladies and gentlemen, the beautiful should die young, let others live as long as they can. However, ninety-five per cent of humanity get their parts wrong. Beautiful women live into their eighties, ugly men die at twenty-two. It's farcical. I'm an actor so I don't mind playing farce on stage . . . but not off. I'm living a farce and I can't stand it . . . I can't live a life without point or purpose . . . old age, failing powers . . . stupid, stupid . . . Forgive me. Goodbye, forever . . . "

SEI: I didn't think that up myself. I got it from some book or other and dressed it up in my own style.

REN: I didn't know that.

SEI: I was always doing it. Other people's words became my words. Poets, playwrights, philosophers, I turned their words into mine. They were my words as soon as I said them, my ideas, my feelings. When I was young it was easy. But it got more difficult as the years passed. The words didn't become mine, they escaped, there was a gap between them and me. The more I struggled the more I lost control of them . . . That retirement speech was terrible. They weren't my words. It wasn't what I wanted to say, would've said, if I'd used my own words. Why did everyone get so excited?

REN: Because it was an exciting moment.

SEI: Sister . . .

REN: Sister?

[SEI *puts his arm around* GIN'*s shoulders.*]

SEI: I can tell you the truth because you're my sister. That last night of *Othello* was a gamble. If my speech had really touched the hearts of the audience, I wouldn't have retired. If they'd've shouted "No! . . . No!" I would've run straight back into those spotlights. But when I got to "Forgive me . . . Goodbye forever" all they did was clap! They were glad.

GIN: No.

SEI: And after the applause the stupid questions. Why is he retiring? Can he still act? Is it true his legs are almost paralysed? . . . My gamble failed.

GIN: You're tormenting yourself on purpose. The theatre was filled with cries of people asking you to stay.

SEI: I didn't hear them.

GIN: Because you didn't want to.

[SEI *quickly moves away from* GIN *and crosses to* REN.]

SEI: All right, I'm not going to change my mind but the least I can do is listen to what you have to say. After all, you've come a long way . . .

REN: I'm waiting for Mizuo.

SEI: Who's that?

REN: You know who it is. You asked her to come.

GIN: Ren, please!

REN: Nawa Mizuo — the actress! You couldn't've forgotten her.

SEI: No, no, of course . . . I always wanted to act with her.

REN: What are you talking about? She acted with you hundreds of times . . . I did too.

SEI: You acted with me?

REN: Often. You could easily've forgotten me. But Mizuo was different. She played opposite you . . . You can't have forgotten, you're putting it on. It's just another brilliant bit of acting! It is, isn't it?!

GIN: No need to get excited.

SEI: It's all my fault . . . my memory isn't what it was . . . I didn't mean to confuse you . . . what you're trying to say is that you want to bring this actress Mizuo and me together on the stage.

REN: What?

SEI: And I've just realised something . . . You're in love with her, aren't you?

REN: Of course I am. That's why I'm here.

SEI: I knew it.

REN: And another thing. Mizuo is now a great star. Every appearance on stage is an event.

SEI: Well, she's lucky to be around at the right time. These days all the best parts are written for actresses. Nobody in Japan wants to see actors past forty. It's a young man's game but actresses can go on forever. They're always in season.

REN: It's got nothing to do with seasons. She's brimming over with talent. It's unique, wonderful. What would you know about it? You haven't been on a stage for three years. You gave up, quit, dropped out — just keep your damn mouth shut.

SEI: Come on, don't get so worked up . . .

REN: I'm sorry . . . I just feel like that about her . . . and I didn't sleep at all last night. I'll get something to eat.
  [REN *exits, stage left.*]

GIN: He was very rude.

SEI: In a way he's right. What do I know? I have been away from the stage for three years. But I have to say, his eyes are cruel . . . cruel eyes . . . I'm hungry.

GIN: I'll get you something.
  [*She moves away then turns back and makes the familiar hand signal.*]
  Hello . . .

[SEI *does not react.* GIN *exits, stage left.*]

SEI: I wish I had a mirror so I can see my face . . . that's stupid . . . just a stupid habit . . . [*quoting*] "I'm just one of the crowd, like a leaf left from last summer" . . . or like a peacock with a bare bottom . . . A what? . . . A peacock with a bare bottom . . . not a peacock again! I'm obsessed with peacocks . . .

[*Two fifth-form schoolchildren,* TAMAMI *and* TOUTA, *in white, appear in the darkness of the seats behind* SEI.]

TAMAMI: Sei! . . . Sei! . . . You'd better give it back!

TOUTA: Can you hear us?

SEI: Yes, but what do you want me to give back?

TOUTA: The peacock.

SEI: What peacock?

TAMAMI: The one you stole from the science lab — I saw you.

TOUTA: Me too. And I saw the peacock fly. What a sight!

TAMAMI: It must've been. That peacock was stuffed! Sei jumped from the window with it.

TOUTA: So Sei was flying as well as the peacock.

TAMAMI: Don't be stupid.

SEI: If that's the way Touta saw it, that's the way it was . . . I'll give the peacock back later, when all the fuss has died down.

TOUTA: When's that?

SEI: I don't know!

[TAMAMI *and* TOUTA *vanish and* UNCLE KAMIHIDA *appears behind* SEI.]

Who's that?

KAMIHIDA: Your Uncle Kamihida . . . "The shrieks of the peacocks at the time were like steel blades tearing across the sky in all directions. Green feathers scattered everywhere. And each of those tiny feathers were like countless tiny peacocks, stained with green brilliance, as the first rays of the morning sun rose over the distant hills . . . " That's a passage from my favourite novel, *Peacocks*. I've read it so many times I know it by heart. Reading that novel makes you feel more attracted to peacocks than when you actually see them in the flesh . . . Hadn't you better put that stuffed one back, Sei? I worked things out last night with your School Principal. Don't worry, I once suppressed evidence in a rape case he was involved in so he was very anxious to help. If you return it quickly there'll be no questions asked . . . nothing. You may think it's a lot of fuss about one stuffed bird. Actually, the Principal said something of the same thing last night. "Well, Mr Kamihida, we all do things like that when we're young." I grabbed him by the throat and yelled, "No, we all don't! I never stole a penny. Never!" . . . It's true, Sei, I never have. I couldn't do any dishonest act now, even if I wanted to. It's engrained. It's my great limitation as a human being.

SEI: But, Uncle, you threatened the teacher — that's not honest.

KAMIHIDA: He deserved it. Complete villain, that man! . . . I don't understand life . . . or things like justice and injustice . . . I'm going to leave the police in five years' time. Frankly, you can't work properly if you worry about things like justice and injustice.

[*The sound of laughter as* UNCLE KITAHIDA *and* COUSIN NISHIHIDA *appear out of the darkness and march down the aisle carrying large bundles on their shoulders and whistling.*]

SEI: Who's that?

KITAHIDA: Your Uncle Kitahida.

NISHIHIDA: And your Cousin Nishihida.

KAMIHIDA: What do you think you're up to? Drunk this early in the evening! If you weren't relatives of mine I'd've locked you up long ago.

KITAHIDA: On what grounds? Because we're drunk?

KAMIHIDA: No, for selling those jackets. They're defective. When they get wet they fall to pieces. We've been flooded with complaints.

KITAHIDA: They've got no reason to complain. We tell every

prospective buyer these are genuine, one hundred
per cent 'seconds'.

NISHIHIDA: Absolutely genuine.

KITAHIDA: That's why we're selling 'em so cheap.

NISHIHIDA: Cheap? We're giving them away.

KITAHIDA: We can't say where we got them, but they're a steal.

NISHIHIDA: That's right, we stole them.

KITAHIDA: Buy whilst stocks last. Everyone expects 'seconds'
to fall to pieces. That's the way we do business.
We're pedlars, Hidahama pedlars, and we're proud
of it.

NISHIHIDA: Feel that? . . .

KITAHIDA: What is it?

NISHIHIDA: It's starting to rain.

KITAHIDA: Quick, cover up the jackets or they'll fall to pieces
in front of his eyes.

NISHIHIDA: No, it's all right, he's gone.

[UNCLE KAMIHIDA *has already disappeared in the
dark, upstage.*]

KITAHIDA: What was he saying to you, Sei?

NISHIHIDA: It was about the peacock, wasn't it?

SEI: How do you know?

NISHIHIDA: When he came to see the Principal we were trying
to sell him a jacket, so we hid behind a screen and
heard everything.

KITAHIDA: Sei, I've got to tell you, your Uncle Kamihida is the
odd man out in Hidahama. You know we've always
been famous for producing actors, pedlars and
con-men — we're men with silver tongues. But
your Uncle Kamihida is a *policeman*! It's unheard
of. He's the black sheep of the family.

NISHIHIDA: He's not all bad. He did tell the Principal everyone
in our family loved beautiful things. That's why you
were fascinated by the peacock.

KITAHIDA: I still don't understand it. There's not much money
in stealing a stuffed peacock.

NISHIHIDA: He didn't steal it for the money.

KITAHIDA: Why then?

NISHIHIDA: Ah . . . Well, that's Sei's secret, isn't it?

KITAHIDA: Oh yes . . . fair enough.

[MIZUO *is standing, like a white shadow, at the back, upstage centre.*]

NISHIHIDA: Secrets are secret.

KITAHIDA: If you touch a secret it melts . . . people with secrets shimmer.

NISHIHIDA: What's that mean?

KITAHIDA: You're right . . . time we went home. A couple of days in Hidahama'll get our feet back on the ground . . . Hey, what's that? . . . Something just flew past.

NISHIHIDA: A shooting star . . .

KITAHIDA: No . . .

SEI: That was my peacock.

NISHIHIDA: Is that a joke?

SEI: No

KITAHIDA: Are you ill?

SEI: Don't argue! It was the peacock, I tell you! It's ready to fly again . . . somewhere in the darkness . . . I'm sure of it!

[COUSIN NISHIHIDA *and* UNCLE KITAHIDA *vanish upstage to be replaced with* YOUTHFUL FIGURES *in white shirts amongst the rows of seats.*]

[SEI *finally notices* MIZUO *as she comes downstage to him. The* YOUTHFUL FIGURES *disappear and* GIN *enters unnoticed, stage left.*]

Where did I put that peacock? . . . I hid it somewhere . . . I can't remember . . . I'm sorry but this cinema is closed . . . no films tonight . . .

[SEI *exits, upstage.* GIN *comes forward.*]

GIN: Hello.

MIZUO: I got a letter from him. He said he was drowning . . . and he had to see me . . .

GIN: I know. I wrote it.

MIZUO: That's a lie. It's his writing. I recognise it. I've had letters from him before.

GIN: I wrote them too. I wrote all his letters.

MIZUO: **What?**

> [MIZUO *tries to leave but* GIN *catches her by the arm.*]

GIN: **Listen to me . . . please!**

> [*The lights fade out.*]

Scene Three

Thirty minutes later. A shaft of light. SHIGEO *and* REN *enter, upstage centre, jostling each other as lights gradually fade up.*

SHIGEO: **All right, all right, you don't have to shove.**

REN: **I'm not shoving. I'm just walking behind you.**

SHIGEO: **Then why don't you walk somewhere else?**

REN: **You don't think I'm lying, do you? She is here. A woman in a white dress . . . She told me.**

> [NOBUKO *has entered, uneasily, upstage centre.*]

SHIGEO: **Keep out of this, Nobu.**

NOBUKO: **I haven't said anything yet.**

REN: **Just tell me where she is.**

SHIGEO: **All right, she was here, but she left by the back exit. Isn't that right, Nobu?**

NOBUKO: **Yes.**

REN: **You're hiding something!**

SHIGEO: **No, we're not.**

REN: **Yes, you are — look at her face.**

SHIGEO: **Did you see something, Nobu?**

NOBUKO: **Madame Gin and the woman from Tokyo were talking in the other building.**

REN: **Take me there!**

SHIGEO: **Stop pushing!**

> [*At that moment* MIZUO *enters, stage left, pursued by* GIN.]

GIN: **But I've still got things to tell you.**

> [NOBUKO *exits.*]

MIZUO: **I don't want to hear.**

REN: Are you all right? What happened? . . . Did you see him?

MIZUO: Sei didn't write those letters.

REN: Who did? . . .

[MIZUO *looks across at* GIN.]

His wife?

[GIN *sits down.*]

What's this all about?

GIN: I was just trying to explain to her . . . Shigeo, did you hear something?

SHIGEO: Like what?

GIN: A scream . . .

SHIGEO: No, but I'll take a look.

[SHIGEO *exits, stage left.*]

GIN: I wanted her to come here for his sake. You've seen the state he's in. We've been here three years and he's getting worse. He rejects people . . . especially those he knew in Tokyo . . . he's almost wiped them completely from his memory . . . I've been forgotten too!

REN: Impossible.

GIN: He thinks I'm his sister. His sister died ten years ago . . . The only thing he doesn't forget is that he's an actor . . . unfortunately. Though he's never going back on the stage he still plays to an imaginary audience. Then just a month ago he started seeing a peacock flying in this cinema.

REN: A peacock?

GIN: Nobody else sees it, of course. But a few days ago he climbed that pillar to catch it, lost his footing, and nearly killed himself . . . [*to* MIZUO] At least you believe the story about the peacock, don't you?

REN: Is that why you forged the letter to get her down here?

GIN: I was clutching at straws. I'll try anything to get him to react . . .

REN: So you want to use Mizuo as a stimulant — shock tactics?

GIN: I haven't the energy to explain . . . too tired to find the right words. I just need your help.

REN: I know about clutching at straws . . . but this is stupid . . . [*to* MIZUO] Why don't you say something?

MIZUO: Darling, don't you see how frightening this woman is? She terrifies me. It's just what you'd expect from a former actress — quite a performance . . . But I'm not going to be used again . . . certainly not as some kind of stimulant.

REN: I know, I know! Don't let's talk about it. That's what we agreed when we got married, remember?

MIZUO: Yes, I'm sorry . . . but she'll sacrifice anyone for his sake . . . she reeks of other people's blood . . . Let's go home!

REN: Right away.

[SHIGEO *enters, stage left.*]

SHIGEO: I can't find him anywhere.

REN: He's probably playing with his peacock.

GIN: I'm worried. He could hurt himself.

[*She exits, stage left, with* SHIGEO.]

REN: I didn't mean what I just said . . . I'd better go and look for him too.

[*He exits, stage left.* MIZUO *is conscious of someone looking at her. She turns upstage.* SEI *appears out of the darkness.*]

SEI: I've just remembered, you didn't come here to see a film, did you?

MIZUO: No.

SEI: Is there something you wanted to speak to me about?

MIZUO: No . . .

SEI: Then I've got it wrong . . .

MIZUO: Wait . . . we've met before.

SEI: Yes, a little while ago.

MIZUO: No, before that. We met a long time ago.

SEI: Did we? I hope you don't mind me asking but are you an aspiring actress?

MIZUO: I was when I visited your dressing room for the first time.

SEI: I suppose I said something very pompous. Like . . . "Acting is a profession that demands sacrifices."

MIZUO: Yes, you said something like that.

SEI: Oh dear. Did I say anything else?

MIZUO: You told me not to live too long. You were sick of eighty-year-old beauties. Theatre was for the young.

SEI: So's life. I must've used that cliché thousands of times . . .

MIZUO: You also said if I wanted to be a good actress I'd have to have an all-consuming love affair.

SEI: What drivel. It's embarrassing. All-consuming love affair . . . I really said that?

MIZUO: Yes!

SEI: There were some lines like that in a play I did once . . . I never acted just to earn a living. I knew too much about myself, I got sick of being me, so I acted. I turned myself into characters that weren't me, so I had to lie to myself. Because I'm a coward I played a hero, because I'm a scoundrel I played a saint, because I'm alone I act. It's because I love the truth but have a horror of the truth that I act. It's because I knew if I didn't act I'd go mad, so I act. Now I don't . . . You really don't have to have an all-consuming love affair . . . you didn't take that advice, did you?

MIZUO: Yes. I had an all-consuming love affair three years ago.

SEI: Three years ago?

MIZUO: When I was alone with my lover for the first time I felt . . . light as a feather . . . But I remember thinking it was all very strange. It should've been happy . . . but I was sad and as time went on I became sadder.

SEI: Yes, the beginning of love can be very sad . . . Who was your lover? No, don't tell me. I don't want to know . . . He wasn't an actor, was he? I mean you couldn't have been so foolish as to fall in love with an actor.

MIZUO: I did.

SEI: Oh damn, too late then. Tell me what happened between you two. No, no, that's too direct. It'd be more romantic if I ask you in what sort of places did you meet.

MIZUO: We both liked walking. So whenever we met we used to go for walks.

SEI: Walks . . . that's very ordinary.

MIZUO: We used to like discovering streets we hadn't walked down before. We even bought a street map of Tokyo so we could study it together.

SEI: A street map of Tokyo. That sounds fun . . .

MIZUO: He liked steep roads . . . and narrow streets with steps . . . He loved going down side streets with narrow passages and a few steps at the end . . . and once we'd climbed them we'd always find wide roads at the top . . .

SEI: He sounds like a man who likes to make it hard for himself and everybody else . . . or maybe somebody who wanted to get to the top . . .

MIZUO: In the middle of the night he'd sit down in one of those alleys and talk.

SEI: Right under one, forlorn, street lamp . . .

MIZUO: That's right. It would always be under a street lamp for some reason.

SEI: He was an actor . . . he always made sure to choose the right setting. Actors do that. They can turn an ordinary street into a stage. What happened after those walks? You couldn't have wandered around forever.

MIZUO: Yes we did. We often kept walking until dawn.

SEI: What energy . . . How old was he? . . . Older than you, I'll bet . . .

MIZUO: Yes.

SEI: **Married?**

MIZUO: Yes.

SEI: So that's why he took you walking all night.

MIZUO: At dawn, when it was time for us to go, he'd take me into some empty street and go through the same ritual.

SEI: Ah, ritual . . .

MIZUO: He'd perform a play for me . . . just for me alone . . . "Goodbye . . . this is our last goodbye . . . we remain true to ourselves to the end . . . we tried to resist oppression and injustice and we failed . . . but there's honour in that failure. Now we wait for our end . . . to be taken out and shot . . . yet I feel so calm. I can hardly believe how calm I feel . . . Someone is playing a tango far, far away."

SEI: Stop! Who are you? What're you plotting against me?

MIZUO: Plotting?

SEI: You're quoting from a play I did when I was young! . . .

MIZUO: Why are you so upset?

SEI: You're right, it's ridiculous. It's just lines from a play. I don't own them . . . I'm tired. Just tell me how your all-consuming love affair ended . . .

MIZUO: Badly. It was all a lie. Those three months together . . . lies. He was deceiving me. It was all an act.

SEI: Love and acting go together. If an actor's in love, no matter how dull he usually is, he'll perform a little better — not that much, but a little.

MIZUO: What he did was terrible. He was jaded. So he used me to revitalize himself.

SEI: Did he tell you that?

MIZUO: No, his wife did.

SEI: What has his wife got to do with it?

MIZUO: She planned it all, and smiled all the time she was telling me. "I'll do anything — I don't care who I hurt to give him back his youth and brilliance as an actor."

SEI: They both sound mad. How can anyone get back

their youth? It's over. Gone forever. <u>Terrible, but it</u>
<u>has to be faced</u> . . . Mind you, trying to get back his
brilliance as an actor . . . I admire that . . . Yes . . . but
why did she tell you? Was it because something
unexpected happened so she had to stop the fake
affair? . . . I know . . . he fell in love with you for real.

MIZUO: That's a lie!

SEI: No, it's the truth.

MIZUO: If it is, why would he forget me? Why would he go
mad?

SEI: I don't want to hear any more!

MIZUO: Look at me. That man I was talking about was you . . .
I was in love with you!

SEI: You're the one who's mad! This woman is mad!

[*As* SEI *pushes* MIZUO *aside, she collapses on the
floor.* SEI *turns back to her.*]

Are you all right? . . .

[SEI *lifts her up in his arms and hugs her.* GIN
and REN *enter, upstage centre, and stare at
them.*]

There . . . there . . . it's hard loving such a terrible
man . . .

[*A thin shaft of red light, then all lights fade
out.*]

END OF ACT ONE

ACT TWO

Scene One

Sound of a gale outside. The curtain in front of the doors, stage right, billows open, as if blown by the wind. Dark FIGURES *enter, carrying a door on their shoulders. On the door is the dripping wet body of a* WOMAN *who has just drowned. Leading the improvised funeral cortege are* UNCLE KITAHIDA *and* COUSIN NISHIHIDA.

KITAHIDA: Right, put her down there.

NISHIHIDA: Careful! . . .
  [*They put the door down.*]

NISHIHIDA: Shall we try some more artificial respiration?

KITAHIDA: It's no use . . . it's over . . . Isn't she beautiful?

NISHIHIDA: I used to think the Hidahama family had the most beautiful woman in these parts. But this one's better . . . especially wet.

KITAHIDA: Yes . . . it's true . . . Come closer, you'll get a better look.
  [*The other* FIGURES *only sigh.* SEI *wakes up.*]

SEI: What's happening?
  [UNCLE KITAHIDA *crosses to him.*]

KITAHIDA: Your sister's dead.

SEI: What?

NISHIHIDA: She jumped off the North Beach pier . . . They tried to rescue her but it was too late.

KITAHIDA: Sei, you'd better take a last look at her.
  [*As* SEI *shakes his head in horror,* UNCLE KAMIHIDA *enters, stage left.*]

KAMIHIDA: All right, carry her to the police station.

NISHIHIDA: What for?

KAMIHIDA: There'll have to be a post mortem, you idiot.
  [*Grumbling to themselves, the* FIGURES *pick up*

*the door, with the corpse, and exit slowly,
stage right.* SEI *stares fixedly at the ground.*]
Why did she drown herself?

NISHIHIDA: Her husband was late coming home.

KAMIHIDA: Late coming home? He's a seasonal worker, isn't
he?

NISHIHIDA: He came back later than planned.

KAMIHIDA: How much later?

NISHIHIDA: Three days.

KAMIHIDA: Three days! Who the devil drowns themselves
because of a three day delay?

KITAHIDA: She did. Does it bother you?

KAMIHIDA: Yes . . . three days. All for three days.

NISHIHIDA: Well, she had a very fiery temper.

KAMIHIDA: Very fiery . . .

KITAHIDA: The women of Hidahama are noted for their fiery
tempers. They're descended from that woman who
jumped into the sea with little Antoku in her arms.

KAMIHIDA: Little Antoku? Who's that?

KITAHIDA: Little Antoku — the Emperor Antoku, of course. The
one who drowned during the Battle of Dannoura . . .
You remember he's supposed to have said,
"Where're you taking me, Grandmother?" The
woman turned to her Emperor and said, "Into the
depths of the ocean. That's where you'll find a
palace waiting for you." And with those words she
jumped into the sea with him and was never seen
again.

KAMIHIDA: But that's a legend of the Taira clan. I've heard tell
the people of Hidahama were all descended from
the Minamoto clan.

NISHIHIDA: The Minamoto clan? Really, I never knew that.

KAMIHIDA: Clan legends are really messy. You don't know
where you are. But it all still doesn't answer why
Sei's sister couldn't've waited for another week or
so . . .

KITAHIDA: I don't know.

KAMIHIDA: No, I suppose not . . . Three days?

NISHIHIDA: Three days.

KAMIHIDA: Three days!

NISHIHIDA: Three days.

> [UNCLE KAMIHIDA *exits, stage right.* COUSIN NISHIHIDA *puts his arm around* SEI's *shoulder.*]
> Don't lose heart.

KITAHIDA: That's right, don't lose heart. Your sister didn't. I mean, there was nothing half-hearted about throwing yourself into the sea like that . . . Mind you, it was a bit hasty. Just three days and 'splash', in she goes.

NISHIHIDA: In a way I can understand why Kamihida goes on about it.

KITAHIDA: Mind you, the people of Hidahama were always doing things like that . . . You remember that legend . . . long, long ago, when they were all running away from the Battle of Dannoura and they ended up collapsing on the beach. It was night and they believed they were safe until some idiot thought the sound of waves was an attack by the enemy. He yelled, "We're surrounded. Run for your lives!" So everybody rushed about like headless chickens. Half of 'em disembowelled themselves and the rest drowned.

NISHIHIDA: We're a panicky lot.

KITAHIDA: Same thing happened, long, long ago at the Battle of Ujigawa. They heard a flock of ducks taking off in the distance, thought the enemy was being reinforced, and started running in a blind panic.

NISHIHIDA: It's in the blood.

KITAHIDA: The people of Hidahama are the stuff of legends — the wrong ones, of course . . .

NISHIHIDA: But it doesn't matter, so long as we can keep our heads above water.

KITAHIDA: And not get too confused by the sound of the waves.

> [UNCLE KITAHIDA *and* COUSIN NISHIHIDA *exit, stage right, laughing.*]

[*Lights full up.* SEI *gets up as* GIN *enters, stage left.*]

SEI: I dropped off. How is she?

GIN: She'll be all right after a good night's sleep.

SEI: I shouldn't've shouted . . . but she had an attack of madness.

GIN: She was worried about you.

SEI: Me? Why?

GIN: Because you seemed so disturbed . . . You shouldn't sleep here without a blanket.

SEI: I had a dream. You died.

GIN: I did?

SEI: Yes, my sister died and was carried in on a door. I couldn't look on your face, I was too scared.

GIN: How did your . . . I die?

SEI: Your husband's return home was delayed three days so you jumped into the sea.

GIN: Because of three days?

SEI: Yes, in my dream they went on and on about it. They said she was too hot-blooded . . .

GIN: If you decided to die it makes no difference if it's because of three days or three decades. It's all the same when something goes to pieces inside a woman . . . I envy her . . . I'd like to swap places with that dream sister of yours . . . Time for us to go to bed . . .

SEI: Yes . . . but do you mind if I look in on that young woman? . . .

[GIN *glares.*]

Just a peep . . . I won't if you . . .

GIN: Don't wake her.

SEI: Good . . . Just a peep, then . . . Didn't you feel . . . the madness inside her . . . it had a strange sparkle . . . I wonder what it is? . . .

[SEI *exits, stage right.* GIN *turns downstage.*]

GIN: I understand what he's talking about. That strange sparkle . . . He has it and I'm dazzled by it . . . It's the sense of danger that clutches the heart . . . It looks like he's started falling in love with her again. As if he'd met her for the first time . . . Am I ready for such pain? . . . I can't pretend it's not happening. After all, I planned it like this.

[*Lights out.*]

Scene Two

The following afternoon.

Lights up on REN, *drinking and eating in one of the seats. He is surrounded by beer cans and take-away food.*

SHIGEO *enters, upstage centre.*

REN: [*offering him a beer*] Want one?

SHIGEO: I don't drink during the day.

REN: Don't be so unfriendly. Keep me company.

SHIGEO: All right. I'll have a bun.

REN: No, I've only got two left. Have some fried chicken.

SHIGEO: No thanks. I'm only trying to be friendly.

REN: So have some chicken.

SHIGEO: I want a bun.

REN: Have a banana.

SHIGEO: It's a bun or nothing.

REN: But I told you there's only two.

SHIGEO: I'm not asking for two. I just want one.

REN: But they're different. One's filled with chocolate and the other with custard.

SHIGEO: Keep them. I don't want any now.

REN: Good . . . How's my wife?

SHIGEO: She's still on the sofa in the office. Why don't you go and see her yourself?

REN: No, not with your damn brother clinging to her like a leech.

SHIGEO: You're taking the train back to Tokyo this evening, aren't you?

REN: We were, but now it's no good. We should've taken the train back yesterday.

SHIGEO: It's none of my business but why aren't you a bit more assertive?

REN: How can I be when I have my doubts about everything? . . . Love, marriage, friendship . . . I'm a realist. I never had any great expectations of this marriage. I knew things had happened in the past between Mizuo and your brother. Anyway, I'm not her type. I married her because I thought I could provide a safe place for her . . . some kind of peace. My friends said it was a case of Beauty and the Beast but I didn't mind. It certainly didn't turn out for the best . . . Looking back, it seems both of us gave good performances in a play called 'Marriage'. What do you think?

SHIGEO: I don't know.

REN: Everything's a performance, you're performing now.

SHIGEO: I'm not!

REN: Everybody looks as though they're acting to me.

SHIGEO: Isn't it important for an actor to be full of doubts?

REN: Now you're making fun of me . . .

[NOBUKO *enters, stage right, with a box of food.*]

NOBUKO: It's for him.

SHIGEO: More food?

REN: When I'm unhappy I can't stop eating — don't laugh.

[HANA *enters, stage left.*]

HANA: The cherry blossoms are starting to fall. If it gets any colder we won't be able to tell the difference between the blossoms and the snow . . . What's all this food? Can I have some?

SHIGEO: Don't touch the buns.

HANA: Why not? I like buns.

REN: I'm going outside . . . find some quiet spot so I can eat alone.

[*He picks up as much food as he can and exits, stage left.*]

NOBUKO: Don't forget this lot.

[*She runs after him with the box of food.*]

HANA: Why's he still here?

SHIGEO: Lots of reasons . . . You said on the phone you had something urgent to tell me.

HANA: Remember yesterday I said the construction work would take place this summer. Well, it looks like we're starting a bit earlier.

SHIGEO: When?

HANA: Middle of May.

SHIGEO: But that's next month!

[SEI *enters quietly, upstage centre. The others do not notice him.*]

HANA: The sooner we open the supermarket the better.

SHIGEO: But I haven't told Sei about it yet.

HANA: When you do, tell him the truth, that you're selling the cinema because it's deep in the red . . . We've got a firm offer from Hokuriku Construction so it doesn't much matter what Sei says . . . Right, I've got things to do. Oh yes, I almost forgot. Kayo says she wants to cook something special for you, so come over.

SHIGEO: What about that other matter?

HANA: What other matter?

SHIGEO: Nobu . . . I'd like her to work with me in the supermarket. I asked you about her before.

HANA: When did you ask?

SHIGEO: A couple of days ago . . . It's all right, isn't it?

HANA: No.

SHIGEO: What? What do you mean, no? Her sight isn't what it was but she can still do odd jobs about the place.

HANA: Maybe. But I don't want her.

SHIGEO: Why?

HANA: Why are you going to so much trouble for her?

SHIGEO: Because . . . well . . . she's worked here a long time . . .
         Why're you so difficult about her?

HANA: Because you are . . . Let me put it this way, my Kayo
         really cares for you — even if she is a bit over-
         weight.

SHIGEO: A bit! . . . Anyway, that's got nothing to do with this.

HANA: Yes it has.

SHIGEO: I see. Very well, if that's the way it is I shall have to
         reconsider selling this place.

HANA: You must be joking!

SHIGEO: I mean it.

HANA: You'd risk the whole thing just because of that girl?
         You must be out of your mind!

SHIGEO: Oh I am, am I? Get out!

HANA: No, I'm staying!

SHIGEO: I said, get out!

        [SEI *crosses to them.*]

SEI: Shhhh . . .

        [HANA *and* SHIGEO *start.*]

HANA: I didn't see you there.

SEI: Shhh, she's asleep.

SHIGEO: She sleeps a lot.

SEI: She's exhausted. If you watch her you can see her
         taking deep breaths and then sinking back into a
         deep sleep as though she was diving into the sea . . .
         and swimming down to the bottom of the ocean
         . . . and the land of dreams . . .

SHIGEO: You seem very cheerful. How long have you been
         sitting there?

SEI: Only a short time.

HANA: In that case you probably overheard us. The fact is,
         I've decided to buy the Northern Metropole. I
         intend to turn it into a supermarket.

SEI: That's the obvious thing to do with it. Nobody
         comes to see films any more. The building's useless.

HANA: You see, Shigeo, you worried too much. Sei is very
         understanding. So stop making things difficult.

SHIGEO: If you accept the position about Nobu . . .

HANA: Impossible!

SHIGEO: Then go to hell!

SEI: Shhh.

HANA: Sei, don't you think he's out of his mind? Losing his head over a girl like that.

SEI: What girl?

HANA: Nobu — the cleaner.

SEI: Oh her, I think she's gloomy, compared with my Sleeping Beauty.

SHIGEO: What did you say?

SEI: I said I think she's gloomy.

SHIGEO: Nobody asked for your stupid opinion!

HANA: How can you talk to your brother like that?

SHIGEO: My brother! Don't make me laugh. I call him my brother because I can't think of a word to describe him. He leaves home suddenly in his teens and comes wandering back thirty years later . . . What right have you to call her gloomy? There's nobody more gloomy than you.

SEI: A moment ago you said I was cheerful.

SHIGEO: But overall you're gloomy! Despite the fact you've had it easy all your life.

HANA: What do you mean?

SHIGEO: He leaves home when he pleases and wanders back when he feels like it. We'd all like to do that, wouldn't we? You could say I didn't have the guts to do it but that's not really true. Everyone has the chance sometime but it depends on luck if we pull it off. It's only a chosen few who get the chance to leave their families. The rest of us have to stay on — like me . . . and Nobu. I won't let anyone call her names!

HANA: All right, that's enough.

SHIGEO: No it isn't! When he finally comes back, you'd think he'd try to behave like a brother. No chance. It's like living with someone from another planet.

HANA: But your brother's ill.

SHIGEO: So am I! I need help. Why can't we ever talk things over?

HANA: Talk? What do you want to talk about — girls?

SHIGEO: Well, yes . . . What's wrong with talking about girls? Brothers are the best people to talk about girls with. But he won't . . . he won't talk about anything. And he has the gall to call her gloomy. Gloomy!

HANA: Don't keep saying 'gloomy' all the time. Have you tried hard enough? Talking with him, I mean.

SHIGEO: Of course not. Just look at him. Standing there bolt upright, his nose in the air, looking up at a sky that isn't there . . . How can anyone talk to him?

SEI: You should try.

SHIGEO: What?:

SEI: I think you should try.

SHIGEO: Oh, shut up!

> [SHIGEO *hits out at* SEI, *who immediately puts up his fists. They circle each other and exchange blows as if in a boxing ring.*]

HANA: Stop it!

SHIGEO: Keep out of this!

HANA: Sei, stop fighting.

SEI: Shut up, you old cow!

HANA: Right, you can both go to hell . . . be as crazy as you like! This bloody rotten cinema's making you all ill. The sooner we tear it down the better.

> [HANA *exits angrily, stage left. As soon as she is gone they stop fighting.*]

SHIGEO: It's like we were kids again . . .

SEI: Is my nose really in the air?

SHIGEO: No . . . only sometimes . . .

SEI: I think I'm a bit more awkward than I seem.

SHIGEO: I'd say that . . .

SEI: Do you really fancy Nobuko?

SHIGEO: Yes.

SEI: You have to admit she is gloomy.

SHIGEO: Yes, she is, isn't she?

SEI: But you don't mind?

SHIGEO: No.

[NOBUKO *enters, upstage centre, looking neat and well-dressed.*]

NOBUKO: Is it all right if I go out shopping for an hour or so?

SEI: Go ahead.

[NOBUKO *exits, stage left.*]

Why don't you go shopping with her?

SHIGEO: Me?

SEI: Remember the last scene of *Casablanca* where Bogart says to Bergman, "You're getting on that plane with him. If you don't go you'll regret it. Maybe not today, maybe not tomorrow, but soon and for the rest of your life . . . "

SHIGEO: [*imitating Bergman*] "But what about us?"

SEI: [*imitating Bogart*] "We'll always have Paris . . . "

SHIGEO: [*imitating Bergman*] "Here's looking at you, kid."

SEI: No, that's my line . . . [*imitating Bogart*] "Here's looking at you, kid."

SHIGEO: But what has *Casablanca* got to do with me going shopping? . . . Oh, it doesn't matter.

[SHIGEO *hurries off after* NOBUKO, *stage left.*]

[*Lights fade.*]

SEI: My body's warping . . . My brother's had it hard . . . my fault . . . Not my fault . . . Other people used to talk like my brother . . . They'd say, "Art is an act of rebellion." . . . "You ran away." . . . Listen, can you hear them? . . . Listen . . . "You used us." . . . "We are being crucified." . . .

[*The voices of* TAMAMI *and* TOUTA *are heard.*]

TAMAMI: [*off*] Sei! . . . Sei! . . .

TOUTA: [*off*] Where's the peacock? . . .

TAMAMI: [*off*] Yes, the peacock . . .

SEI: Shut up! Shut up!

[UNCLE KAMIHIDA *appears in the half-darkness, upstage.*]

KAMIHIDA: Sei . . .

SEI: No, I don't want to hear anything. Get out! Now . . . now . . .

[UNCLE KAMIHIDA *bows respectfully and disappears upstage.*]

Calm down . . . Nobody can act well if they're upset . . . I'll sleep for a while. Sleep puts an end to things . . . [*suddenly assuming the role of Hamlet*] "To die, to sleep; to sleep: perchance to dream: ay, there's the rub; for in that sleep, blah, blah, blah, blah, blah, blah" . . .

[MIZUO *enters, stage left.*]

You must take it easy. At least sit down.

MIZUO: Thank you. I've put you to a great deal of trouble.

SEI: Who're you looking for?

MIZUO: Ren.

SEI: Oh, the one who's always eating.

MIZUO: We're going back to Tokyo this evening.

SEI: This evening? . . . Why're you in such a hurry?

MIZUO: We're going home.

SEI: Is he your manager?

MIZUO: Manager?

SEI: A strange man. Last night, when you were lying on the sofa and I was sitting beside you, he came in and gave me a banana. And this morning he gave me an orange. Does he think I'm suffering from a vitamin deficiency? Of course, it's very generous of him but he doesn't give them generously, he thrusts them into my face like this, as if he were angry.

MIZUO: Did you take them?

SEI: Yes. He has a strange power, it was as if I had to take them. But they weren't easy to eat . . . Wait a minute. Let me get this clear in my head. The man you told me about yesterday, your lover, he's not the vitamin man, is he?

MIZUO: No. Two different people.

SEI: What happened to the other one — the one who took you for walks?

MIZUO: Well . . . I don't know . . .

SEI: What's the matter? Yesterday you were talking about him with such passion.

MIZUO: Yes, but afterwards I realised he's past history.

SEI: Is that true?

MIZUO: Yes.

SEI: I'm glad to hear it.

MIZUO: Are you?

SEI: Yes. I've been worrying about it all morning. It's very sad you getting so upset about a man like that . . . what time's your train?

MIZUO: Four o'clock.

SEI: Do you really have to leave today?

MIZUO: Yes.

SEI: There isn't much time . . . Let's walk to the top of the cliffs. Around here there are some wonderful steep roads.

MIZUO: Steep roads?

SEI: I've walked them all. If you stop, turn round and look down, you can see the Sea of Japan below . . . It's the end of winter now . . . it looks very strange . . . all veiled in mist . . . thousands of white strands that float like smoke above the water . . . You look down, into the mist, and see nothing has shape or substance and it seems that the world is coming to an end . . . Come on, you can see for yourself . . .

MIZUO: No.

SEI: Why? Don't you like steep roads?

MIZUO: No, I hate them!

SEI: Oh, yes . . . I just realised that must've brought back very painful memories. The man who took you for walks liked steep roads, didn't he? . . . That was very insensitive of me, I'm sorry.

MIZUO: I shouldn't've got so hysterical.

SEI: No, it's my fault. It's a bad habit of mine getting other people mixed up with myself . . . it's been getting worse lately. Better if I just shut up and let you talk. Tell me something interesting . . .

MIZUO: Me?

SEI: Like the dream you had this morning that made you sweat so badly.

MIZUO: Oh that . . . I dreamed of a bird circling very slowly in the sky . . .

SEI: A bird? What colour? Was it a peacock?

MIZUO: No, I don't think so . . . it didn't seem to have any colour to speak of . . . it just kept circling.

SEI: Is that it?

MIZUO: Yes . . .

[TAMAMI *and* TOUTA *are heard in the distance.*]

TAMAMI: [*off*] Sei! . . .

TOUTA: [*off*] Sei! . . .

SEI: Will you shut up!

MIZUO: What?

SEI: Sorry, but they're such a nuisance . . . Let's talk some more . . . I've never had any trouble with talking. I've given a three-hour monologue on stage, and when I was young I used to talk with friends days and nights without a wink of sleep . . . Now I'm not so sure. It's not that I don't have anything to talk about . . . I have all sorts of memories and I know some very funny stories too . . . The problem is I don't really know if the stories really happened to me or to somebody else . . .

[*The figures of* UNCLE KITAHIDA *and* COUSIN NISHIHIDA *appear dancing, upstage, in the half-light, casting huge shadows.*]

Go away, damn you! . . . [*to* MIZUO] Let's shake hands.

MIZUO: What?

SEI: Shake hands . . . You see, if we do, maybe the man I used to be . . . maybe that man will go straight to your heart without any need of words . . . I wonder which play those lines came from? Too good for me just to have made them up. Oh never mind, let's shake hands.

[SEI *holds out his hand.* MIZUO *backs away.*]

Don't you like shaking hands?

MIZUO: It's not that. When he ran out of things to say he used to offer to shake hands.

SEI: Who did?

MIZUO: You! I mean the man I went for walks with.

SEI: Oh, he used to run out of things to say, did he? I never pictured him like that. I got the impression he must've been very eloquent. Didn't you say he used to sit down on some steps in the middle of the night and talk about the theatre?

MIZUO: Yes, in the beginning.

SEI: But it changed later, did it?

MIZUO: Yes, at first he was wonderful . . . sharp, sophisticated . . . like those attractive, older men you see in films . . . Actually, he was just pretending to be like that . . . acting! After a time he became very quiet . . . he looked as though he was fighting some terrible unseen fear. I couldn't bear it. I told him I didn't understand what was happening but I wanted to help . . .

[SEI *sniggers.*]

What's so funny?

SEI: That's a trick men often use . . . appealing to a woman's maternal instincts.

MIZUO: Is it?

SEI: Are you angry?

MIZUO: I've no way of knowing if he was really sick or if it was just a trick like you say. During the last week he hardly talked at all. We just walked in silence in the night and when morning came we just bowed briefly to each other, turned our backs . . . and went home.

SEI: Walking in silence . . . all night . . . if that was a trick it was amazingly daring . . . acting out the part of a silent, tortured hero. But it doesn't sound like a trick. He couldn't have been that good an actor. Don't overrate him.

MIZUO: If that's right . . . and he wasn't acting when he was with me . . . then his feelings were real . . . true . . .

SEI: We came to the same conclusion yesterday. He did love you after all . . . Are you going to say it isn't true again?

MIZUO: No . . . it's true. I was too young to recognise it then . . . I shouldn't've believed what his wife said . . . he did love me . . .

[MIZUO *cries.*]

SEI: It's all too late now, of course. In which case your love should be pitied too. In my opinion he was to blame. He was too weak, both as a man and as an actor. In the end I think he'd have to give up acting and disappear . . . You shouldn't think of things from the past . . . it's dangerous. Let me see the sparkle in those eyes again . . .

[*He embraces her.*]

I have this strange feeling . . . as though I've held you like this before . . . somewhere . . . at dawn . . . in a mist . . . No, no, it can't be true . . . I've got it all wrong. There isn't much time, is there? Weren't you with someone? Oh yes, the vitamin man. Who is he? Do you love him? It doesn't matter. We'll meet again soon, I'm sure of it . . . I'd like to give you a memento of our meeting . . . I know what . . . It's a play I did with some friends when I was young. I'll do the opening lines for you . . . "Goodbye . . . this is our last goodbye . . . we remain true to ourselves to the end . . . "

MIZUO: Stop it!

SEI: Sorry . . . I didn't mean to . . . I've done it again, haven't I? I told you to forget the past and now I've made you remember that man . . . I didn't mean to hurt you. It's all over . . . What a fool I am!

[SEI *crouches.* MIZUO *goes to him.*]

MIZUO: Forgive me. Go on.

SEI: No.

MIZUO: Please.

SEI: No.

MIZUO: In that case, I will . . . [*quoting*] "Goodbye . . . this is our last goodbye . . . we remain true to ourselves to the end. We tried to resist oppression and injustice and we failed . . . but there's honour in that failure. Now we wait for our end . . . to be taken out and shot . . . yet I feel so calm. I can hardly believe how calm I feel . . . Someone is playing a tango, far, far away . . . "

[*A tango is played as she continues.*]

"I see so many scenes . . . a white road in morning mist . . . newspapers driven by the wind like fallen cherry blossoms . . . lights someone forgot to turn off . . . the school drinking fountain . . . and the boys in shirt sleeves, drinking water from a cup on a chain . . . and those figures there . . . it's . . . those who loved me then . . . "

[MIZUO *holds out her arms to* SEI, *who resists for a moment. But he then puts his arm round her waist and they dance the tango.*]

[REN *enters, stage left, with a new bag of food. He puts down the bag and glares at the dancers.*]

[*When the dance has reached its climax* SEI *leads* MIZUO *to* REN, *as if entrusting her to him. While* MIZUO *and* REN *dance* SEI *goes up the aisle, upstage centre.*]

[MIZUO *and* REN *stop dancing.*]

[GIN *appears out of the darkness, upstage, where she has been watching them.*]

[*As* SEI *reaches* GIN *he holds out his hands and sinks into her arms.*]

[*Lights fade out.*]

Scene Three

Ten minutes later.

Lights up on MIZUO *in one of the seats, dressed ready for a journey.*

SHIGEO *and* NOBUKO *enter, stage left, laughing.*

SHIGEO *crosses to* MIZUO.

SHIGEO: Where's your husband?

MIZUO: He's gone to find out what time the train leaves.

SHIGEO: That's a pity. I had a feeling we could've hit it off.

NOBUKO: [*clutching shopping bags*] I'll go and put these away.

SHIGEO: Fine, fine . . . Don't run.

[NOBUKO *exits, stage left, just as* REN *enters.*]

REN: The five-fifteen express is just right. It's via Maibara, then pick up the bullet train at Nagoya for Tokyo . . . We're leaving after all.

SHIGEO: I can see.

REN: Thanks for everything. I really would like to have seen a film in this cinema. Any plans to reopen it?

SHIGEO: No, it'll probably be pulled down next month.

REN: Well, we'd better be off.

SHIGEO: It's too early if you're taking the five-fifteen. You'll just have to wait at the station.

REN: Perhaps it's better if we wait here then . . . No, we'll go. [*to* MIZUO] Come on! . . . [*to* SHIGEO] Give our regards to your brother and his wife . . . Bye . . .

[*They are just about to leave when* GIN *enters, stage left.*]

SHIGEO: Gin, you've come just in time. They're catching the five-fifteen.

GIN: It's snowing. The roads're turning white.

SHIGEO: It's started already, has it?

GIN: Shigeo, get a couple of umbrellas for them.

REN: No, that's all right.

SHIGEO: I'd better. The snow around here is very wet.

[SHIGEO *exits, stage left.*]

GIN: I have to thank you . . . Sei has come back to me for the first time in years . . . when we embraced he even called me by my name . . .

REN: Did he?

GIN: Yes, didn't you hear him?

MIZUO: No.

GIN: He did. You look as though you don't believe me . . . Well, maybe you're right, his voice was so low I couldn't really catch what he said. Maybe he called me by my name or maybe he just called me 'sister' like he's done till now . . . I don't care much either way . . . I'm Gin, the wife of Kiyomura Sei . . . Then again, perhaps Gin the wife is only a character in a play which I have to keep playing no matter what. Anyway, I've decided to accept the role I've been given, whether it's Gin the wife, the sister or neither . . . Just so long as he knows I'll always be there to catch him when he falls . . .

[*A loud humming is heard upstage as* SEI *comes out of the darkness, carrying a large net.*]

Darling . . .

[*But* SEI *is totally indifferent to everyone as he looks along the rows of seats, searching for something.*]

[SHIGEO *enters, stage left, with two umbrellas and sees* SEI's *behaviour.*]

SHIGEO: What is it? What's he doing?

[SEI *continues to prowl around the seats.*]

GIN: I don't know.

SHIGEO: Sei . . .

GIN: Listen, darling . . .

SEI: Shush, I can't concentrate.

SHIGEO: What're you looking for?

SEI: The peacock. The peacock I stole thirty years ago. I finally remembered I hid it somewhere. All these years I'd forgotten about it but I know definitely it's hidden somewhere around here.

SHIGEO: That's ridiculous. It can't be here.

SEI: Shush!

> [*The voices of* TAMAMI *and* TOUTA *are heard out of the darkness.*]

TAMAMI: [*off*] Come on Sei! Quick . . .

TOUTA: [*off*] Let's see it! Quick . . .

TAMAMI: [*off*] Sei . . .

TOUTA: [*off*] Sei . . .

SEI: Shut up! I'm going to find it any minute now . . .

> [UNCLE KITAHIDA *and* COUSIN NISHIHIDA *appear out of the darkness, upstage centre.*]

NISHIHIDA: Secrets are secret.

KITAHIDA: If you touch a secret it melts . . . People with secrets sparkle . . .

NISHIHIDA: They really do.

KITAHIDA: Forget the peacock, Sei.

NISHIHIDA: It's not worth it.

KITAHIDA: It's a strange-looking bird.

NISHIHIDA: Especially if you look closely.

SEI: Leave me alone!

> [SEI *charges at them but they evade him.*]

NISHIHIDA: Secrets are secret . . .

KITAHIDA: People with secrets sparkle . . .

SEI: Stop it!

KITAHIDA: Time we were off . . .

> [*As they march off into the darkness* UNCLE KAMIHIDA *appears in their place.*]

SEI: You too!

KAMIHIDA: Yes, but I'm going to talk to you first. No, I'm not going to give you advice. I'm just going to tell you a secret — just one. And I've never told it to anyone else before . . . I once stole a peacock myself . . . and from the same science lab that you did. It was a long time ago, of course. You don't believe me, do you? But it's true. So we're very much alike you and me . . . Let's shake hands . . . If we shake hands your youth will enter into me . . .

SEI: Get off me! Get off me!
    [*Voices out of the darkness.*]

TAMAMI: [*off*] Sei . . .

TOUTA: [*off*] Sei, listen . . .

SEI: It's here! It's here! I've found it! I've found the peacock!
    [SEI *pulls out a dirty cushion from under one of the seats. He seems to think it is the stolen peacock as he hugs it tightly.*]
    My precious . . . Oh, my precious . . .

GIN: [*low to* SHIGEO] My precious? What's he talking about?

SHIGEO: It's madness.

SEI: See, I've found it! . . . I've found the peacock! . . . What's the matter, why don't you come and look at it? . . . Are you afraid? Because it looks strange? . . . It isn't strange, it's beautiful . . . Look at the dark, blue feathers round its neck . . . and the light green ones there . . . and this faint emerald line . . . so delicate . . . so beautiful . . .

GIN: It's all over. If I were dealing with a human being there'd still be hope. But I'm not and now it's over. I give up, my part as the wife, the sister and all the other parts I've played too . . . No more parts . . . I refuse to play any more parts. All the years I've spent with him . . . the days of pain and happiness . . . is this how it ends?
    [*She turns and exits, stage left.*]

MIZUO: Wait . . . Well, I won't give up!

REN: Mizuo . . .

MIZUO: No, I'm going to tell him it isn't a peacock. Why hasn't someone told him? What're they afraid of? It isn't a peacock, it's a dirty old cushion!

REN: Mizuo, don't!
    [*But* MIZUO *pulls herself free of* REN's *grip and goes up to* SEI.]

MIZUO: Throw that thing away.

SEI: Thing? What thing?

MIZUO: Please throw it away.

SEI: You're joking.

MIZUO: It isn't a peacock, it's just a dirty old cushion.

SEI: No! How can you call such a beautiful bird an old cushion? . . . Look at it, look at that beautiful emerald colouring round the neck.

MIZUO: It's a dream! Wake up!

[*She snatches the cushion from* SEI.]

SEI: You're mad! Go to hell!

[*He pounces on* MIZUO *in a fury, grabs her round her neck and strangles her.* REN *leaps on him and tries to drag him off* MIZUO *but* SEI *continues strangling her.*]

Down, strumpet! Nay, if you strive, Desdemona . . .

[*As* MIZUO *stops struggling* SEI *releases his grip and looks down at her in bewilderment.*]

Mizuo? . . . It is Mizuo, isn't it? . . . What happened?

[REN *takes the body of* MIZUO *from him and lays her down gently.*]

REN: You maniac! You've killed her!

SEI: No . . . no . . . keep calm . . . It was only a play . . . What was it? . . . *The Cherry Orchard*? . . . *Hamlet*? . . . No, of course it was *Othello* . . . the last scene of *Othello* . . . I've just strangled Desdemona, haven't I? . . . What's next? . . . Exit, lights down, curtain, applause . . . No, no, there's something else . . . Yes, the announcement of my retirement . . . that's very important . . . Keep cool . . . this is my last performance.

[*He acknowledges imaginary applause.*]

Ladies and gentlemen, in life the beautiful should die young, while the others can live as long as they like. Unfortunately, ninety-five per cent of people get it all wrong. Beautiful women live into their eighties and ugly men die at twenty-two. Life is unpredictable and a farce. As an actor I like playing farces but I hate living them . . . So I bid you farewell.

Goodbye ... this is our last goodbye ... we remain
true to ourselves to the end.... Wait ... those aren't
my lines, I'm quoting again ... they all get mixed up
. . . I'll try again . . . Ladies and gentlemen, the
connection between a poet and his age is not
merely a reflection of that age but also of the
invisible part of it . . . No, that's no good either.
Those are lines from a bad play I did twenty years
ago ... I don't own my own words any more ...
but please believe me, ladies and gentlemen, my
feelings towards you are still here, deep in my heart
... it beats for you ...

[*The strains of a tango are heard.*]

Listen, listen, I can really hear a tango ... here ...
now ... I break through these thick walls that crush
me, so at last I can put my arms round my love ...

[*As* SEI *dances with an invisible partner,* REN
rushes and stabs him. SEI *staggers but continues
dancing.*]

[*Dark* FIGURES *multiply out of the darkness
and dance together: they are people from* SEI*'s
dreams.*]

[*Suddenly a section of the cinema caves in
and a great wind blows in cherry blossom
and snow.*]

[*The tango reaches its climax.* SEI *stops dancing
and collapses without a sound. At that
moment we see a peacock in flight.*]

[*Lights out.*]

Scene Four

Lights up on GIN *in a coat.*

GIN: If I'd been here would I have called that dirty
cushion a peacock or would I have had the guts like

Mizuo and called it a dirty cushion? . . . I don't think
I was able to behave as madly as him any more . . .
but who knows? . . . This place is going to be pulled
down in May as planned . . . It's a beautiful, sad
place, isn't it? . . . That's why he made his home here
. . . beautiful and sad . . . beautiful and sad . . .

> [*The dark* FIGURES *enter in slow motion. They
> applaud and cheer as if they had just seen a
> film.*]

> [*Lights slowly fade out.*]

THE END

Q   What do the following have in common:
Steven Berkoff · Michael Burrell ·
Anton Chekhov · Brian Clark ·
Barry Collins · Eduardo de Filippo ·
Keith Dewhurst · Nell Dunn ·
Charles Dyer · Rainer Werner Fassbinder ·
Donald Freed · Maxim Gorky ·
Richard Harris · Ronald Harwood ·
Roy Kift · Hanif Kureishi ·
Bob Larbey · Tony Marchant ·
Sean Mathias · Mark Medoff ·
Julian Mitchell · Mary O'Malley ·
Caryl Phillips · Manuel Puig ·
James Saunders · Anthony Shaffer ·
Martin Sherman · August Strindberg ·
Peter Terson · Heidi Thomas ·
Brian Thompson · John Wain ·
Hugh Whitemore · Snoo Wilson ·
David Wood · Sheila Yeger ?

A   They're all playwrights, silly!

Q   But what *sort* of playwrights?

———————→